Stranger Danger

Bully on Campus & Online

Drugs & Alcohol

Gunman on Campus

Natural Disasters

Navigating Cyberspace

Peer Pressure & Relationships

Protecting Your Body: Germs, Superbugs, Poison, & Deadly Diseases

Road Safety

Sports

Stranger Danger

Terrorism & Perceived Terrorism Threats

Stranger Danger

Christie Marlowe

Mason Crest

Mason Crest
450 Parkway Drive, Suite D
Broomall, PA 19008
www.masoncrest.com

Printed and bound in the United States of America.

First printing
9 8 7 6 5 4 3 2 1

Series ISBN: 978-1-4222-3044-2
ISBN: 978-1-4222-3054-1
ebook ISBN: 978-1-4222-8838-2

Library of Congress Cataloging-in-Publication Data

Marlowe, Christie.
  Stranger danger / Christie Marlowe.
      pages cm. – (Safety first)
  Includes index.
  Audience: Ages 10+
  Audience: Grade 4 to 6.
  ISBN 978-1-4222-3044-2 (series)—ISBN 978-1-4222-3054-1 (hardback)—ISBN 978-1-4222-
8838-2 (ebook) 1. Children and strangers–Juvenile literature. 2. Kidnapping–Prevention–
Juvenile literature. 3. Safety education–Juvenile literature. I. Title.
  HQ784.S8M373 2015
  613.6071–dc23
                                                      2014003855

Contents

Introduction

No task is more important than creating safe schools for all children. It should not require an act of courage for parents to send their children to school nor for children to come to school. As adults, we must do everything reasonable to provide a school climate that is safe, secure, and welcoming—an environment where learning can flourish. The educational effectiveness and the strength of any nation is dependent upon a strong and effective educational system that empowers and prepares young people for meaningful and purposeful lives that will promote economic competitiveness, national defense, and quality of life.

Clearly adults are charged with the vital responsibility of creating a positive educational climate. However, the success of young people is also affected by their own participation. The purpose of this series of books is to articulate what young adults can do to ensure their own safety, while at the same time educating them as to the steps that educators, parents, and communities are taking to create and maintain safe schools. Each book in the series gives young people tools that will empower them as participants in this process. The result is a model where students have the information they need to work alongside parents, educators, and community leaders to tackle the safety challenges that face young people every day.

Perhaps one of the most enduring and yet underrated challenges facing young adults is bullying. Ask parents if they can remember the schoolyard bully from when they were in school, and the answers are quite revealing. Unfortunately, the situation is no better today—and new venues for bullying exist in the twenty-first-century world that never existed before. A single bully can intimidate not only a single student but an entire classroom, an entire school, and even an entire community. The problem is underscored by research from the National School Safety Center and the United States Secret Service that indicates that bullying was involved in 80 percent of school shootings over the past two decades. The title in this series that addresses this problem is a valuable and essential tool for promoting safety and stopping bullying.

Another problem that has been highlighted by the media is the threat of violence on our school campuses. In reality, research tells us that schools are the safest place for young people to be. After an incident like Columbine or Sandy Hook, however, it is difficult for the public, including students, to understand that a youngster is a hundred times more likely to be assaulted or killed at home or in the community than at school. Students cannot help but absorb the fears that are so prevalent in our society. Therefore, a frank, realistic, discussion of this topic, one that avoids hysteria and exaggeration, is essential for our young people. This series offers a title on this topic that does exactly that. It addresses questions such as: How do you deal with a gunman on the campus? Should you run, hide, or confront? We do not want to scare our children; instead, we want to empower them and reassure them as we prepare them for such a crisis. The book also covers the changing laws and school policies that are being put in place to ensure that students are even safer from the threat of violence in the school.

"Stranger danger" is another safety threat that receives a great deal of attention in the modern world. Again, the goal should be to empower rather than terrify our children. The book in this series focusing on this topic provides young readers with the essential information that will help them be "safety smart," not only at school but also between home and school, at play, and even when they are home alone.

Alcohol and drug abuse is another danger that looms over our young people. As many as 10 percent of American high school students are alcoholics. Meanwhile, when one student was asked, "Is there a drug problem in your school?" her reply was, "No, I can get all the drugs I want." A book in this series focuses on this topic, giving young readers the information they need to truly comprehend that drugs and alcohol are major threats to their safety and well-being.

From peer pressure to natural disasters, from road dangers to sports safety, the Safety First series covers a wide range of other modern concerns. Keeping children and our schools safe is not an isolated challenge. It will require all of us working together to create a climate where young people can have safe access to the educational opportunities that will promote the success of all children as they transition into becoming responsible citizens. This series is an essential tool for classrooms, libraries, guidance counselors, and community centers as they face this challenge.

Dr. Ronald Stephens
Executive Director
National School Safety Center
www.schoolsafety.us

Words to Know

instincts: Behaviors that are part of our own nature, not requiring any thought.
vandalize: Cause damage to property (a house, store, or land, for example).

Chapter One

Real-Life Stories

Raul grew up in a big city. He knew only a few of the many people living and working in the city by name. This means that most of the people around him every day were strangers, people he didn't know. Most strangers aren't dangerous. Most of them are people just like you and deserve your kindness and respect. But a few strangers can be dangerous. They may want to harm or kidnap young people. And it can be hard to tell the difference between someone who means well and someone who doesn't. This is no reason to be afraid of every stranger you see. But as Raul would learn, danger is a good reason to put your safety first!

LEARNING STREET SMARTS

When you grow up in a city, there are a lot of people to see, many places to visit, and lots of ways to get around. When Raul was young, he wasn't allowed to leave his apartment without one of his parents. His parents knew strangers can be dangerous. And even if there were no dangerous people out there, city streets would still be very dangerous places for a young child.

When Raul was twelve, his parents started letting him leave the house by himself. They let him walk to school, walk around his neighborhood, and sometimes visit friends if they lived nearby. But he always needed his parents' permission to leave the house. They always needed to know

Most people you pass on the street have no interest in trying to hurt you, but it's still safest if you avoid conversations with them.

10 **Stranger Danger**

exactly where he was headed and when he would be home. Now, getting to leave the house alone was a whole new freedom Raul had never known.

But this new freedom came with a new responsibility. "Raul must understand how dangerous strangers can be," his parents said to each other. They decided it was time to sit Raul down and make sure he understood how important it was to stay safe when he left the house.

"We trust you a lot," Raul's mother said to him, after explaining they wanted to talk about what it means to be street smart. "It is other people that we don't trust. It's not because they don't deserve our trust. Most of them do. We just want you to know what to do if you get in a dangerous situation."

"Finding yourself alone on a street is an example of a dangerous situation," Raul's father explained. "It's best if you walk around with one of us or with a few of your friends. But even a street with a few strangers is much safer than being all by yourself. This is because most strangers would never dream of hurting you. Most of them just want to mind their own business. And most people would call the police if they saw a young person being hurt or kidnapped."

Someone who is street smart knows what situations she can handle and what situations she can't. Being honest with yourself about the danger that you might be in is also a part of being mature. An immature person might think she could fight off someone who was trying to kidnap her. But in most cases, this isn't true. The best way to stop an attacker is by running and screaming as loudly as you can. But the best defense against these attacks is by staying out of situations where they are more likely to happen.

"Only let grown-ups help grown-ups," Raul's mother said. "Helping people is good, but helping strangers can be dangerous. Saying no to other grown-ups is okay. And if you feel in danger, scream or ask another grown-up for help."

The last thing Raul's parents told him was to trust his **instincts**. Instincts are the part of being human that tells us how to react and feel in a certain situation. If you are walking down a street alone at night, your instincts might make you feel scared and tell you to walk more quickly to get you off that street. There may be no one dangerous around you, but your instincts would be telling you it was a dangerous situation. As Raul's parents told him, you need to be afraid of situations, not people.

RAUL IGNORES HIS PARENTS' ADVICE

Raul listened closely while his parents told him what it means to be street smart. But he didn't take their advice very seriously. He felt old enough to be able to tell if he were in a dangerous situation. And Raul felt he could defend himself if anything dangerous were to happen to him.

A few months later, Raul's close friend, Jacob, invited Raul to spend Halloween night at his house. Raul quickly agreed, knowing that Jacob lived in a neighborhood just outside of the city, which made it a much better place to go trick-or-treating.

Halloween was on a Saturday. Raul's parents rode with him on the train out to Jacob's neighborhood. On the train ride, Raul's parents spoke to him again about being safe and smart while out that night. Raul occasionally said, "OK," as if he had heard what they were saying. But Raul was

Halloween is a night when lots of kids and their parents are out on the streets. It might seem safe to be out, but you should still be careful.

Stranger Danger

You should also be very careful about people who come to your door—especially if your parents aren't home.

far too excited about the night ahead to worry about being safe. He may have heard, but he wasn't listening.

That day, Raul and Jacob had a lot of fun. They worked on their costumes and played some games in Jacob's backyard. Before they went trick-or-treating, Raul and Jacob were joined by a few of Jacob's friends from school. Jacob's parents thought their neighborhood was safe, and no one would bother a group of boys on Halloween night. They told the boys to be back by ten o'clock at the latest—and to be safe.

The group of boys spent most of the evening trick-or-treating. But as the day turned into night, Raul found out Jacob's friends had something else in store for the night. The boys had found out the address of their school principal. Their plan was to egg and toilet paper her house. Raul didn't

A person might seem friendly, but you shouldn't ever get into a vehicle with someone who you don't know.

Stranger Danger

Strangers Aren't the Only People Who Kidnap Young People

Most young people who are kidnapped are not taken by strangers. In fact, they are taken by a parent or someone they know. According to the most recent statistics on kidnappings in the United States, only about one hundred young people are kidnapped by strangers every year. On the other hand, over 250,000 young people are kidnapped by a parent or someone the young person knows. When two parents are separated or divorced, one parent may kidnap their child from the other.

feel comfortable vandalizing the home of someone he didn't know. But he eventually gave in, not wanting the other boys to think he was scared or uncool.

Before long, the boys found their principal's home and began to throw the eggs and toilet paper they had with them. Raul joined in with the other boys at first. But after a short while, he felt too guilty to continue and returned to the street, where he watched Jacob and his friends. What the boys didn't know was that their principal had been watching them **vandalize** her property and had called the police.

A few moments later, a police car turned the corner. The police officer turned on the car's sirens and lights to let the boys know they had been caught. But Jacob's friends would not give up that easily. "Run!" one of Jacob's friends shouted, and the pack of boys sprinted away.

Raul was scared and confused. He turned and ran as fast as he could, hoping he wouldn't get caught. Before long, he lost sight of the police officers. But he had also lost sight of Jacob and his friends. He was alone on the street in an unfamiliar neighborhood.

He began walking back in the direction that he came, hoping to find one of Jacob's friends or an open store, where he could ask directions. He walked for a long time, getting more and more lost with every turn he took.

A short while later, a car turned the corner in front of Raul and drove past him. He didn't think anything of it, until the car turned around and drove up beside him. The driver lowered his window, and Raul was greeted by a kindly looking man. The man told Raul he was driving around, looking for his dog that had escaped from his home. He asked Raul if he had seen any dogs as he was walking. "No," Raul said, feeling sorry for the man.

"That's too bad," the man replied. "Enjoying your Halloween?" the man asked.

"Not really," Raul replied. Raul asked the man if he knew where Washington Street was, hoping the man would give him directions back to Jacob's house.

"Sure," the man said. "Get in, and I will take you there."

"What about your dog?" Raul asked, suddenly suspicious of the man.

"He will come home eventually," the man said. "He escapes all the time."

"No, thanks," Raul said. "Could you just give me some directions?"

"I don't know the road names that will get you there," the man said. "But if you hop in, I will have you there in only a few minutes."

Just because someone smiles and seems friendly does not mean that he is trustworthy. This man, for example, is probably a very nice person—but to be safe, if you don't know someone, be very careful and never go with him or accept anything he tries to give you.

16

Stranger Danger

Most kidnappings are done by someone the child already knows. Even if a child goes willingly, it's still kidnapping when an adult takes a child away from her home without permission.

"No, that's OK," Raul said. "I will find it myself. I hope you find your dog." Raul began walking ahead of the car, hoping the man would drive off.

"Don't be afraid," the man said after pulling up beside Raul again. "I just want to help."

By now, Raul's instincts were telling him he was in a dangerous situation. He didn't know what to say to this man to make him go away. He didn't understand why this man was insisting on helping him. It is obvious, Raul thought, that I do not want help. Why won't he leave me alone? Raul's instincts told him to run away. But he didn't want to insult the man if he really was only trying to help. After all, he thought, he does seem very nice.

"Really, I am fine," Raul said, beginning to walk a bit faster.

But instead of simply driving off, like most people would, the man pulled in front of Raul, blocking his path. The man got out of the car and approached Raul. "Get in," the man said. "I promise you will be home soon."

If someone does something threatening to you, make sure you tell the police or an adult you trust. Even if you got away safely, that person may try to hurt someone else.

Stranger Danger

Raul knew something was definitely wrong. The man got closer to Raul, which made Raul scream for help. The man grabbed Raul's wrist. Raul tried to pull away but found the man's grip far too tight. Raul kicked and punched the man, but it didn't seem to affect the large man at all. Finally, Raul swung his arm around in a circle and broke the man's grip. Raul ran past him and into someone's backyard. He hopped a fence and continued to run as fast as he could.

Raul didn't even know if the man was chasing him, but he kept running for a long time. He only let himself look back once he had found a main road. There, he used a pay phone to call Jacob's parents. Jacob had already been home for about an hour. Jacob's mother had been worried sick about Raul, and Jacob's father was out in their car, looking for him. Jacob's mother told him she would call Jacob's father and tell him where Raul was.

Jacob's father quickly came to pick up Raul. He told Jacob's father about the close call he had with the suspicious stranger. Knowing the man might try to kidnap or hurt another young person, Jacob's father insisted they call the police.

Not long after they called the police, two officers came to Jacob's house. Raul told them everything that had happened and everything he could remember about the man and the car. "You were right to call," the police officer said. "We will send some cars into the area looking for him." Raul gave the police officer his address and home phone number, just in case they found the man.

Raul had learned some important lessons that night!

Words to Know

encounter: To meet someone or come into contact with them.

Chapter Two

What Makes Strangers Dangerous?

Raul didn't keep himself safe that Halloween night. A bad decision led him to get lost in an unfamiliar neighborhood. But he trusted his instincts enough to know not to get into the car with a man he didn't know—even if the man looked nice and was offering to help. When the man attempted to kidnap Raul, he was lucky enough to escape. But not all young people who **encounter** strangers in dangerous situations are as lucky as Raul. Julia Walsh, a mother of a girl who was kidnapped, knows this all too well.

KIDNAPPINGS

Julia's daughter, Jessica, was kidnapped when she was only twelve years old. "It was the most frightening experience that Jessica has even been through," Julia says. "She has never been the same since."

Jessica was kidnapped after attempting to skip school with a close friend named Chloe. The girls walked to school every morning with two boys from their neighborhood. Julia was friends with the other children's parents, so Jessica and Chloe didn't want the boys to know they planned

21

Running away from home can seem like a good idea to a kid—but it can put him in danger from strangers.

Stranger Danger

There is safety in numbers. If you're going to be out, you'll be much safer if you stick with a group of friends.

on skipping. The four walked to school together, but Jessica and Chloe told the boys they had forgotten something that they needed and to go on without them. The boys went into school, and the girls turned around to begin their day off.

Like Raul, Jessica put herself in a dangerous situation. Her parents didn't know where she was and expected that, like most days, she would be safe walking to school with a group of friends. Jessica told Chloe to wait by a nearby field, while she went home to grab some snacks. Jessica walked home slowly, waiting for her parents to leave for work so that they wouldn't know that she was skipping.

Sadly, she didn't make it home. A man stopped her to ask for directions. But before Jessica knew it, he picked her up and threw her into a nearby car. "Everything happened so quickly," Julia says. "Jessica was too scared to run or fight." The man told Jessica that if she screamed, he would tie her mouth shut.

What Makes Strangers Dangerous?

There are many people on the Internet who lie about their identities and might not be trustworthy. It's just as important to stay safe online as it is in real life!

Stranger Danger

Strangers and the Internet

The Internet is the newest tool strangers are using to deceive young people. "Strangers instant message me at least once a week," admits fifteen-year-old Cara, who knows that Internet safety is important. "The first thing people ask is, 'Where do you live?' and 'How old are you?' I never used to think twice about it, but now I either ignore the question or give a fake answer." Remember, someone you meet on the Internet may seem nice and funny. It may seem you have a lot in common. They may trick you into thinking they have good intentions. In truth, some people use the Internet in the same way some dangerous strangers will ask a young person for help. It is all a way to deceive them into putting themselves into a dangerous situation!

The man drove Jessica back to his home. When he opened the car door, Jessica refused to leave the car. The man grabbed her by her wrists and dragged her inside the house. He locked Jessica in his basement. Jessica screamed and cried, asking for the man to let her go. But the man beat her and told her that if she didn't stay quiet, he would kill her.

Luckily, a neighbor of the man saw him drag Jessica inside his home. The neighbor called the police, saying she had seen some suspicious activity at the man's home. The police arrived after Jessica had been kidnapped for only a few hours. Julia didn't even realize her daughter was anywhere but school.

Jessica heard the police arrive and screamed as loudly as she could. The officers heard the screams and searched the man's home. They found Jessica, bruised and bleeding, in the basement. The man was arrested immediately, and Jessica was freed.

"It was a horrible experience for Jessica," Julia says. "But we really were lucky. If that neighbor hadn't seen the man dragging Jessica out of his car, who knows what he might have done to her."

Since the experience, Julia has become an expert on the dangers strangers pose to young people. She runs programs at schools to teach kids how to stay out of dangerous situations and what to do in if strangers approach them.

"Strangers kidnap young people for many reasons," Julia says. "The two most common reasons are in order to sexually abuse the child or to hold her for ransom." Sexual abuse is when a young person is forced to have sex with an adult. Ransom is when someone is held in order to steal money from the people close to the victim. The kidnapped person is held until a certain amount of money is paid to the kidnapper. Sadly, in both cases, the kidnapped child is often killed so that the kidnappers have a better chance of getting away with their crimes.

In Jessica's case, it is hard to tell what the man planned on doing with her. "But the police do not think it is likely that he planned on ransoming her," Julia says. "I just do not want this to happen to anyone else. Some people might think that bad things happen because of sick or cruel people. They are right. But it is the responsibility of young people to keep themselves safe from these kinds of people. Being angry at the sick or cruel people will not stop them from trying to hurt you or others."

Be responsible with your money. Don't spend it on things you're not sure are legitimate, and don't give away your money without seeing what it is you're buying.

In the old days, a common scam was the one shown here, where bets were placed on which cup held a bean or a stone—and really none of them did. This scam goes all the way back to the days of Ancient Greece! Today, however, Internet scams are far more common.

SCAMS AND TRICKS

"Kidnapping is the most obvious danger that strangers pose to young people," Julia says. "But it is not the only danger that is out there. Sometimes a stranger may want to trick or scam a young person in order to steal from them."

Julia remembers the story of a teenager she heard about. The teenager was visiting a large city with some of her friends. They were spending time on a street with a lot of small stores.

The girls were having a good time, until a stranger approached them. The stranger asked if the girls were interested in buying a fake driver's license. The girls knew that with a fake driver's license, they would be able to buy alcohol, even though they were still a few years too young to buy it legally.

One of the girls agreed, and the stranger told her to follow him. Already the girl was putting herself in a dangerous situation by agreeing to be alone with a man she didn't know. But she wanted to impress her friends by fearlessly doing something she knew was dangerous and illegal. This is an example of how peer pressure can cause us to make bad decisions and put ourselves in dangerous situations.

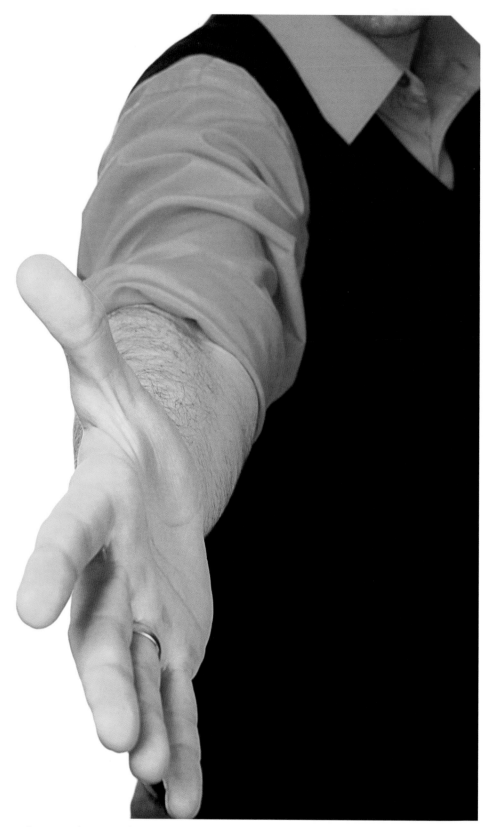

We need to have some amount of trust in the people around us, or society would not be able to function. Some people take advantage of this to get what they want.

Stranger Danger

While they were walking, the stranger told her the fake driver's license would cost $60. It was most of the money she had left. But she handed it over anyway. He pocketed the money and told her they were going to the back room of a store, where the fake drivers' licenses were made. They walked to the back of the shop, and he told the girl to have a seat on a nearby bench. He said he was going to talk to the men he was working with. He pointed down the street and said a man would come out of a shop and wave to her when they were ready.

The man disappeared into the store. The girl waited on the bench for ten minutes before realizing she had been scammed. She returned to her friends, embarrassed a stranger had scammed her so easily.

Luckily, the man only wanted to steal from her. But you can see how much easier it would be for the man to hurt or kidnap the girl after separating her from her friends.

"In most cases," Julia says, "putting your safety first means protecting your body. But it can also mean keeping yourself out of trouble with the law or protecting yourself from people who want to steal from you." The girl who wanted to buy a fake driver's license, didn't protect herself, and she paid the price.

TAKING ADVANTAGE OF A YOUNG PERSON'S TRUST

"Sometimes, young people are kidnapped just because they were in the wrong place at the wrong time," Julia says. "The stranger may try to wrestle a young person into a car or a van. But this is rarely the case. Strangers do not want others thinking something suspicious is going on. And what is more suspicious than a young person begin dragged into a vehicle, while they are kicking and screaming? If a stranger is going to kidnap a young person, he will want the young person to come with him willingly. That way, other people will think nothing wrong or suspicious is happening."

As we saw in Raul's story in chapter 1, strangers sometimes make up false claims in order to talk to young people or to give them a reason to go with them. If a stranger asks a young person for help when he doesn't really need it or lies online, that person is trying to take advantage of a young person's trust.

Trust is when you believe another person is being honest with you. It is an important thing to have. It would be a pretty scary world if we walked around all day not trusting or believing anyone. But having complete trust in everyone can be dangerous, too. Julia already mentioned how dangerous strangers can be. Most young people, however, are kidnapped or abused by someone that the young person knows. These people rely on the hope young people will trust them in order to get them in a dangerous situation or convince them to do something they wouldn't normally do.

There can be real emotional dangers in breaking a young person's trust. The physical dangers of kidnapping and abuse are very real and dangerous. But it hurts just as much to find out you have been lied to or that you trusted someone you shouldn't have. Such an experience can make a person extremely untrusting and afraid of others.

"Cuts and broken bones heal," Julia says, talking about the experience her daughter had after being returned to her. "But the pain of losing trust in others takes a much longer time to heal."

Words to Know

patrolling: Keeping watch over an area.
confident: Sure of yourself.

Chapter Three

Staying Safe and Being Prepared

"Communities are beginning to confront the problem of stranger danger in many ways," says Officer Sienna Laris. Officer Laris is a police officer and has been teaching young people how to keep themselves out of dangerous situations, safe from dangerous people. "Strangers can definitely be dangerous," Officer Laris says, "but staying safe also means considering that young people are most often kidnapped or sexually abused by people they know." According to Officer Laris, we still need to keep an eye out for suspicious people. But young people also need the skills to deal with any adult, not just strangers.

POLICE, NEIGHBORHOOD WATCH, AND OTHER TRUSTED ADULTS

People who help keep any community safe from dangerous people are known as trusted adults. "These are people," Officer Laris says, "who young people can trust when they need help or feel threatened. They are people who have their safety and best interests in mind, no matter what."

Strangers have been a big issue for a long time. But most people now agree that telling young people all strangers are dangerous may not be the best advice. "It can be very unhealthy," Officer Laris says, "to think that all people are scary, dangerous, or out to get you." A young person may find herself alone and in need of help. Sometimes, a stranger is the only person available to help

Not all strangers are dangerous. Some, including crossing guards or other officials, can generally be trusted to help you.

Stranger Danger

An important skill to learn is how to judge what kinds of people can be trusted and which ones can't. If you're going to live your life, it's not realistic to never talk to any adult. After all, you're surrounded by them whenever you go to the mall or a busy city!

the young person. And knowing which strangers are safer than others is an important part of staying safe in these situations.

Not all strangers are dangerous, so don't be afraid to ask someone for help. You don't want to stay in a dangerous situation. But thinking that all strangers are trustworthy isn't the right choice, either. This might lead you to ask for help from a stranger who wants to hurt or kidnap you. "Instead," Officer Laris says, "a young person should understand who are the best people to go to when he needs help." Some examples of strangers who can be trusted in most situations are police officers, crossing guards, and firefighters. If you're in a school, teachers, librarians, and principals can usually be trusted. If you are in a store, ask someone working there for help; they can often be identified by an ID badge. A mother or father who has children with them can also probably be trusted to help a young person out.

"Most of these people can be trusted," Officer Laris says, "but they are still strangers." Officer

Neighborhood watch programs are a good way for regular citizens to help keep their neighborhoods safe, especially in areas that might not have a large police presence.

Stranger Danger

AMBER Alert

The AMBER Alert system is an important program used to find children once they have been kidnapped. The system uses television, radio, transportation signs, and other forms of communication to let a community know a child has been abducted. The hope is that if officials get the message about a kidnapping out to as many people as possible, that someone will have seen or will soon see the kidnapped child. Since police started the program in 1996, over six hundred kidnapped people have been saved from kidnappers.

Laris reminds us young people should still keep themselves safe when asking any adult for help. "It is best if a young person stays in a public place when asking anyone for help. If anyone, even a trusted adult, tries to put you in a situation that seems dangerous, say no, and ask another trusted adult for help."

Police officers are always the best people to ask for help. "Police officers fight every day to keep our communities safe from dangerous people," Officer Laris says. "But they are not alone."

Many neighborhoods now have neighborhood watches that help keep a neighborhood safe from suspicious people and strangers. "Police officers are very important, but they cannot be in all places at all times," Officer Laris says. "This is where a neighborhood watch steps in." These people are not police officers but take on the responsibility of **patrolling** a neighborhood in order to protect it. "The adults in a community generally know who lives in the community and who does not. They know who is a stranger in a neighborhood and who is not."

A neighborhood watch is also important because these community members are very aware of suspicious people and young people in their neighborhoods. "An adult going about her daily life may not be looking out for the safety and well-being of others," Officer Laris says. "But the men and women who serve on neighborhood watches are looking for suspicious people."

According to Officer Laris, a neighborhood can only really be safe if people are aware of others and looking out for their neighbors. Many people do this every day. But the neighborhood watch is an organized group of people who volunteer for the job. They don't just watch out for their neighbors when they can. They watch out for their neighbors, because they consider it an important part of living in a community. "This," Officer Laris says, "makes neighborhood watch members not only trusted adults but also an important part of keeping young people in a community safe."

EDUCATION, AWARENESS, AND PREPARATION

"The people who help keep our communities safe are important," Officer Laris continues. "But they are only one part of keeping young people safe. We also need to prepare young people and their parents for dealing with strangers."

Part of Officer Laris's job as a police officer is to educate young people about how to deal with strangers and other adults. "Most stranger-safety programs today," Officer Laris explains, "try to

By preparing ahead of time, you can have the confidence to deal with a scary situation. Talk to your parents about using a safe word, or figuring out some other way to tell who you can trust.

36   **Stranger Danger**

educate young people about rules they can use for both strangers and people they may know who could be potentially dangerous." But according to Officer Laris, it is also important that young people talk with their parents about the best ways to stay safe.

Officer Laris likes to tell the story of a young man named Robbie, who discussed the dangers of being kidnapped with his parents. His parents did some research and decided one of the best ways to keep Robbie safe was to teach him a "safe word." They told Robbie not to go with anyone unless the person, too, knew the safe word—even if it was someone that Robbie knew. If the person didn't know the safe word, he wasn't a safe person. This simple trick ended up saving Robbie from being kidnapped.

One day Robbie left school expecting to find his mom waiting to pick him up. Instead, a couple approached him. They told him his mom couldn't pick him up that day and that she asked them to pick him up. Robbie asked them if they knew the safe word, and they answered incorrectly. Robbie told them that he couldn't go with them and went back inside the school to find a trusted adult. He spoke to one of his teachers, and she helped him call his mom, who had been running late because of traffic.

"Robbie was prepared," Office Laris says. "And being prepared for these kinds of situations is the best way to be **confident** and fearless, even in dangerous situations. If you are prepared for the worst, you don't have to fear strangers as much. You still need to stay guarded against people who might be more forceful than the couple who tried to kidnap Robbie. But being prepared is the most important part of staying safe."

Words to Know

shrewd: Smart and clever.
anxious: Worried or uncomfortable.

Chapter Four

What Can You Do to Stay Safe?

"**Y**oung people can do plenty of things to protect themselves from strangers and other dangerous adults," says Jeremy Wilkinson. Jeremy goes from school to school, teaching young people about the best way for them to avoid dangerous situations. He also teaches important skills young people can use if approached by individuals who might be dangerous. "Avoiding a dangerous person or situation is always the best choice," Jeremy says. "But sometimes these people and situations are unavoidable. That is why kids need to know what they can do to keep themselves safe."

AVOID AND RECOGNIZE DANGEROUS SITUATIONS

Both Raul from chapter 1 and Jessica from chapter 2 found themselves in very dangerous situations. "There are certain places a young person should do their best to avoid," Jeremy says. Places like the woods or small, dark streets make it much easier for a kidnapper. "And it's best," Jeremy continues, "for a young person to always try and travel with an adult or with a group of his or her friends." It is very unlikely you'll be kidnapped or hurt if there are a lot of people around you. But as we saw in Raul's story, even a large group of young people won't always keep you safe if you are in a dangerous situation to begin with.

39

Almost half of all kidnappings by someone who wasn't a family member involved getting the victim into a cars. Never get into a car with someone you don't know and trust!

Stranger Danger

Places without many people around tend to be more dangerous. A kidnapping can happen without anyone to see it and stop it from happening.

This may seem simple. But Jeremy says that avoiding dangerous situations is more complicated than this. "Most kidnappings take place with the use of a car or some other vehicle. It would be too hard for anyone to just drag a young person a long distance. Someone would notice."

Dangerous people can be very **shrewd** and don't want to be caught. Cars or other vehicles offer these dangerous people a quick and easy way to trap a young person and kidnap them without other people noticing. "It's important to avoid a stranger's car completely," Jeremy says. "If a stranger asks you to look in the car, don't do it. Don't agree to look in the trunk or in the back of a truck or van. Don't put your arm in the window to take something or point to something. Don't agree to come closer to see a pet or to get a toy. If a stranger walks up or pulls up in a car, and you're too far away to hear the person, don't go closer, even if the person waves you over. Just get away. Run the opposite way than the car is heading. Get to a trusted adult as quickly as possible." According to Jeremy, a stranger in or near a car is the most dangerous kind.

Talk to your parents about being prepared and how to tell whether a situation is dangerous.

"Sometimes," Jeremy says, "young people can't help being in situations where they are approached by a dangerous person. In these cases, they need to be able to recognize when they are being asked to do something dangerous by an adult." A situation is dangerous if any adult ever asks you to disobey your parents, do something without permission, or keep a secret; asks for help; or makes you feel uncomfortable in any way.

In chapter 3, we saw how Robbie wasn't in a dangerous situation but was still able to recognize when he was asked to do something dangerous. "Even if the stranger knows your name, don't be fooled," Jeremy says. "There are lots of ways to find out kids' names, even when someone doesn't

Stranger Danger

know them or their families." For example, do you have a jacket or a piece of jewelry that has your name on it? That's an easy way for someone to learn your name.

"Young people don't need to be afraid," Jeremy says. "But they do need to have enough street smarts to keep themselves out of danger and to act safely when they might be in danger."

TALK TO YOUR PARENTS OR A TRUSTED ADULT

A situation that is always dangerous is when your parents or a trusted adult are not aware of where you are. "Make sure an adult always knows where you are and when you will get there," Jeremy says. As we saw in chapter 2, Jessica skipped school and didn't tell her parents. None of the trusted adults in Jessica's life knew where she was. When she was kidnapped, no one had a clue, because they all thought Jessica was safe and sound.

"That story," Jeremy says, "makes clear just how important it is for a young person to talk to the adults in his or her life." Talk with your parents about the best ways for you to keep safe. Your parents or a trusted adult will be able to help you a lot more than you might think.

Your parents and other trusted adults often know a neighborhood or an area much better than you do. Asking your parents to point out people and places in your neighborhood that they know and trust is a good way to be prepared if you ever find yourself in need of help. These places are called "safe spots."

"Safe spots are places where you can stop if you need help," Jeremy explains. They are places like the houses of kids you know, your parents' friends' houses, stores, restaurants, police stations, libraries, and fire departments.

Robbie's story in chapter 3 showed us another good reason to talk to your parents or another trusted adult about how to keep yourself safe. Robbie's story showed us how having a safe word with your parents can keep you safe from adults who lie to gain your trust. But it is also important that you know what your parents expect you to do if you are ever lost. For example, imagine you are shopping with your parents at a large store or mall and suddenly lose sight of them. Finding a trusted adult like a store clerk, security guard, or police officer is a good idea. But it might be easier for a young person to have a plan made with her parents beforehand in case anything like this ever happens.

NO, GO, YELL, TELL

"The last thing that a young person should know," Jeremy says, "is what to do if seriously threatened by a stranger." The most important actions to take in a situation like this can be remembered with four words: no, go, yell, and tell.

"No," Jeremy says, "means that a young person has the right to say no if she is asked or told to do something by an adult, especially if it could be dangerous." Saying no to an adult may seem scary. But in most situations with a stranger, it is the safest thing that a young person can say.

"Go," Jeremy says, "means that a young person should attempt to get away from the dangerous person as quickly as possible. He should run if necessary." According to Jeremy, you should do anything you can to keep away from someone who is putting you in danger.

What Can You Do to Stay Safe?

Some areas have emergency phones, which are usually painted blue or have a blue light. Remember that you can use them or a normal phone to call 911 at any time for an emergency.

44 **Stranger Danger**

Dialing 911

There is one number you can dial and will always find a trusted adult ready to help. This number is 911, and it will put you directly through to the closest police department. Only dial 911 in an emergency. But if you find yourself in any sort of dangerous situation, dialing 911 can be a way to bring some trusted adults right to you.

"Yell," Jeremy says, "means making as much noise as possible, especially if grabbed by an adult or if the adult will not leave the young person alone." If a stranger approaches you and follows you when you try to walk away, yell for help as you run away. If a stranger ever tries to grab you, yell as loudly as you can and try to get away. You can shout things like, "Help! I don't know you!" or "Help! This isn't my dad!" People in the area will hear what's going on and help you, so make plenty of noise.

"Tell," Jeremy says, "means running to find a trusted adult as soon as possible." If a dangerous adult tried to grab you, they might try to kidnap another young person. It is important that you tell a trusted adult what happened to you so that they can call the police.

"Lastly, a young person should also always trust their instincts," Jeremy says. "If they are *anxious* or get that uh-oh feeling, it is probably a good time get out of the area, tell an adult, or call 911." Remember, no one will think you are silly for putting your safety first!

Find Out More

ONLINE

Safety Tips
www.fbi.gov/fun-games/kids/kids-safety

Replacing Stranger Danger with Stranger Safety Kidnapping Prevention for Children, Teens, and Adults
www.kidpower.org/stranger-safety

Do You Know How to Be Street Smart?
kidshealth.org/kid/watch/out/street_smart.html

National Center for Missing and Exploited Children
www.missingkids.com/home

Stranger Danger Quiz
pediatrics.about.com/od/parentingquizzes/l/bl_strngdngr.htm

IN BOOKS

Guard, Anara. *What if a Stranger Approaches You?* North Mankato, Minn.: Capstone Press, 2011.

Hulse, Terra, and Jerry Hyde. *Child Survival Skills: How to Detect and Avoid Dangerous People.* Oakhurst, Calif.: Bentle Books, 2004.

Raatma, Lucia. *Living Well: Safety in Public Places.* North Mankato, Minn.: Child's World, 2004.

Raatma, Lucia. *Staying Safe Around Strangers.* North Mankato, Minn.: Capstone Press, 2011.

Ridenour, Melissa Harker. *What Would You Do? A Kid's Guide to Staying Safe in a World of Strangers.* Terra Alta, W.V.: Headline Books, 2011.

Index

About the
Author & Consultant

Christie Marlowe was raised in New York City where she lives with her husband and works as a writer, journalist, and web designer.

Dr. Ronald D. Stephens currently serves as executive director of the National School Safety Center. His past experience includes service as a teacher, assistant superintendent, and school board member. Administrative experience includes serving as a chief school business officer, with responsibilities over school safety and security, and as vice president of Pepperdine University.

Dr. Stephens has conducted more than 1000 school security and safety site assessments throughout the United States. He was described by the *Denver Post* as "the nation's leading school crime prevention expert." Dr. Stephens serves as consultant and frequent speaker for school districts, law enforcement agencies and professional organizations worldwide. He is the author of numerous articles on school safety as well as the author of *School Safety: A Handbook for Violence Prevention.* His career is distinguished by military service. He is married and has three children.

Picture Credits

discard